IMAGES
of America

RANGELEY
LAKES REGION

HERBERT LEON WELCH. Best known for his mounts of fish that incorporated lifelike poses and realistic painting, Herb Welch was one of the premier taxidermists of the first half of the 1900s. However, Welch was truly a renaissance man. He excelled as a fly fisherman, artist, sculptor, guide, fly tier, baseball player, conservationist, teacher, entertainer, and storyteller. Welch was also a champion fly caster, holding the world-record cast of 154 feet with a five-and-three-quarter-ounce rod. His sporting store in Oquossoc became a mecca for sportsmen visiting the Rangeley Lakes region.

On the cover: Two unidentified fishermen pose with a huge catch of trout in the days before laws limited the number that could be taken.

IMAGES
of America

RANGELEY
LAKES REGION

R. Donald Palmer

ARCADIA
PUBLISHING

Published by Arcadia Publishing
Charleston, South Carolina

Library of Congress Catalog Card Number: 2004101338

For all general information contact Arcadia Publishing at:
Telephone 843-853-2070
Fax 843-853-0044
E-mail sales@arcadiapublishing.com
For customer service and orders:
Toll-Free 1-888-313-2665

Visit us on the Internet at www.arcadiapublishing.com

*This book is dedicated to those who have chronicled over the years,
in word and image, the rich history of the Rangeley Lakes region.*

THE RANGELEY LAKE HOUSE. The hotel era in the Rangeley region reached its height with the expansion of the Rangeley Lake House. Situated on the lakeshore, it offered luxury lodging to guests who expected the very best in fine accommodations. The narrow-gauge railroad delivered guests directly to the stone station in front of the Rangeley Lake House. The hotels and their guests positively impacted the small rural community, both economically and socially.

CONTENTS

ACKNOWLEDGMENTS

It is with much appreciation that the author acknowledges those who have assisted in providing material for this book. Margaret R. Yocom, Ph.D.—the folklorist at the Rangeley Lakes Region Logging Museum and an associate professor in the Department of English at George Mason University, in Fairfax, Virginia—made a major contribution to this book by authoring chapter 4, "Logging the Timberwoods." Peggy drew on her extensive knowledge of the people and nature of logging operations to present some wonderful images and descriptions, providing insight into this important part of Rangeley's history. She would like to thank the following people and organizations for their help with her research: Mary Ellen Barnes, David Calder, Bradford Crafts, the Dead River Historical Society, Edward D. Ives, Clarence Jones, the Maine Forest and Logging Museum, Becky Ellis Martineau, J. Michael Martinez, Kaelin Morin, Richard Morin, Hazen "Ben" Morton, William Nevitsky, the Rangeley Lakes Region Logging Museum, Rodney C. Richard Sr., David A. Taylor, Glen Viles, Elijah "Tiger" White, Wayne White, and Gaylon "Jeep" Wilcox.

Special thanks to Jeanne Bowditch, curator of the Rangeley Lakes Region Historical Society, for her impressive work on early camp life at Kennebago Lake, and Gary N. Priest, vice president of the Rangeley Lakes Region Historical Society, for the information contained in his book *History of Rangeley Hotels and Camps*. Of special note is the defining work of Edward Ellis, *Chronological History of the Rangeley Lakes Region*.

Many of the images have been provided by the Rangeley Lakes Region Historical Society.

Also contributing images for this work are Scott Morton, Joan Frost, and Tom Folsom. The majority of the images are from the personal collection of the author and his wife, Stephanie. The author has also relied on the stories and experiences of many longtime residents of the community to add flavor and context to the history of the region.

The coverage of some aspects of Rangeley's history have, of necessity, been limited, due to the absence of quality images. It is hoped that this work will lead to locating previously unknown images that will further add to the richness of our history.

A MOUNTAIN VIEW HOUSE BUCKBOARD. Guests were picked up at the railroad station in Oquossoc by drivers from all the local camps and hotels. This two-team buckboard is shown delivering a number of guests to the Mountain View House, located on the shore of Rangeley Lake.

INTRODUCTION

For the past 11,000 years, people have been drawn to the Rangeley region of the Western Mountains of Maine to pursue wildlife and the fabled brook trout that grow to trophy size. The first visitors to the region were nomadic aborigines who established camps on Aziscoos Lake. Other Native American groups, including the Abenaki and St. Francis tribes, visited the outlet of Oquossoc Lake (later renamed Rangeley Lake) and the Kennebago River. The first white man to set sight on the Androscoggin Lakes, as they were originally known, was Lieutenant Montresor. In 1760, he and his men passed through the region on their way from Quebec to Topsham. Using old trails, the first settlers, Hoar, Toothaker, Quimby, Bubier, Whitney, and Rowe, arrived in Rangeley and quickly established settlements in the early 1800s.

In 1825, Squire Rangeley, his wife, Mary, and his family arrived in his inherited wilderness area, a portion of which was occupied by the early settlers. The squire exchanged the property at 50¢ per acre for their labor. The village grew rapidly based on its farming and lumbering, with new settlements springing up throughout the region.

In the early 1860s, George Shepard Page caught eight brook trout whose total weight was almost 52 pounds. When word of the huge trout spread to New York, Rangeley was forever transformed from a small rural farming community to a popular destination for sportsmen and sportswomen. The first sports stayed with the local farmers and relied on their assistance in locating and catching the highly prized trout. Thus began the lodging and guiding businesses that were to become integral parts of the community and its economy and continue today. The sudden influx of visitors also required better methods of transportation. The buckboards and rough trails made the trip long and arduous. Soon, steamers plied the lakes, allowing sports to visit Upper and Middle Dams, Kennebago Lake, Mooselookmeguntic Lake, and outlying areas. The famous Rangeley boat was designed to navigate the local waters. Enterprising businessmen recognized the need for improved accommodations, and quickly, primitive camps were replaced by comfortable camps and hotels that catered to sportsmen and their families. Two separate railroads served the region, bringing even more sportsmen and providing access to the area's natural resources.

Stories of the fabulous brook trout, some weighing 11 pounds and more, soon eclipsed the reputations of the fabled Adirondacks and Catskills, but the increased fishing pressure on the wild trout population took its toll. To offset the declining numbers and size of the brook trout, landlocked salmon were introduced in the 1870s. However, their presence dramatically reduced the populations of blueback trout, which provided the forage that enabled the brook trout to reach trophy size. The bluebacks' demise and the ascendance of the salmon meant the brook trout had to share the waters and affection of the sportsmen.

Also arriving at this time were some personalities that were to significantly contribute to the traditions and history of the Rangeley region and the entire community of fly fishermen. Ed Grant, a guide, camp owner, and noted Maine storyteller, did much to establish the Kennebago area as prime location for trout fishing. Cornelia "Fly Rod" Crosby was the first to actively promote the area's fishing and hunting through personal appearances and her writings. Captain Barker ran steamers connecting the newly arrived railroads and the camps that sprang up around Mooselookmeguntic Lake, several of which he owned and operated. In the early 1900s, Herb Welch of the village of Oquossoc used his artistic talents to create lifelike mounts and paintings of the trophy fish caught from local waters. Perhaps the most important personality of the era was Carrie Stevens, a milliner who summered at Upper Dam with her husband, Wallace. Carrie designed and tied beautiful streamer flies that are eagerly sought by collectors around the world. Her renowned Gray Ghost pattern is still fished on lakes and streams wherever fly fishermen pursue trout and salmon.

Woods operations have always been an important economic factor, a source of employment, and a valued tradition in the region, as related by Margaret R. Yocom, Ph.D., a folklorist. Logs were cut and hauled by teams of horses to nearby streams and floated down to the numerous lakes. They were gathered in booms and navigated down the lake to where they could be sped on their way to the mill by the release of dammed-up waters. This dangerous work required skill and daring. With the advent of improved roads and transportation, the river drives ended in the 1970s, but they remain an integral part of the folklore of the region.

In the early 1920s, Rangeley became a destination and a second home for many of the families originally drawn there by the lure of the brook trout. However, they now sought a variety of outdoor experiences. Hotels became grander, offering golf courses, boating, dancing, horseback riding, first-run movies, and an expanded social scene. The visitors became not just customers, but friends and supporters of the theater, library, churches, and infrastructure of the community. While the town grew and prospered, it still retained the friendly atmosphere that made it feel like home.

The advent of World War II brought many changes. People were no longer satisfied with vacationing in one location for the entire summer. The automobile, new roads, and a natural interest in seeing the country brought big changes. Hotels shut their doors and were torn down, the contents auctioned; the steamers were dragged up on shore, left to decay or were burned; and the trains no longer came.

However, the possibility of still landing a trophy trout or salmon, the region's wonderful outdoors sporting heritage and traditions, the advent of golfing, skiing, and snowmobiling, and the breathtaking beauty of the region and its warm inviting community have kept visitors returning to the region. While much has changed, much is still the same. There is a renewed sense of commitment to the environment, outdoor traditions, fisheries, and wildlife to ensure that future generations will know and appreciate the history and values of this small community in the Western Mountains of Maine.

FISHING NEAR MOSQUITO BROOK. The entire family is involved in this fishing outing, reported to be near Mosquito Brook on Richardson Lake. The two youngsters seem to be more interested in the photographer than the large fish that Mom is about to net for Dad.

One

EARLY SETTLEMENT

THE EARLIEST VISITORS TO THE REGION. Approximately 11,000 years ago, Native Americans from the north were attracted to the area by the prospects of harvesting huge brook trout and other game. Artifacts from their visits are still occasionally found when lake levels recede. During the winter of 1760, Lt. John Montresor made an extremely difficult expedition across what we now know as Maine, through the Rangeley region to Topsham, Massachusetts.

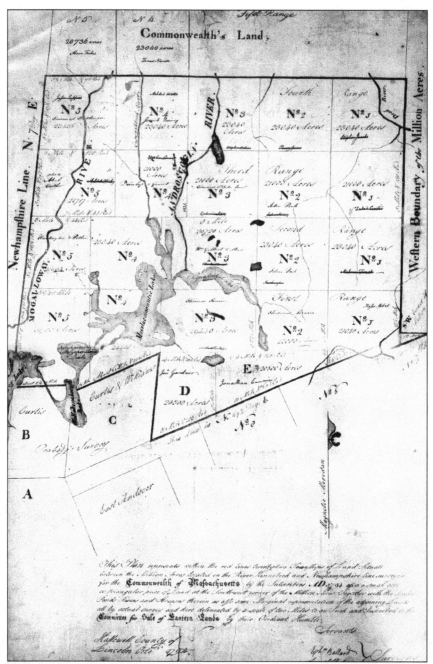

A 1794 MAP. Thirty years later, Ephraim Ballard and Lemuel Perham surveyed the area that was still part of Massachusetts, as shown on their early map. Their system of surveying involved using a grid over the territory all the way to the Canadian border. The grids were approximately 10 miles in width and length. The horizontal strips were termed "ranges," and the overlaying vertical strips were called "townships." The area now known as Rangeley is Township 3, Range 2. The surrounding area was made up of the plantations of Sandy River, Rangeley Plantation, and Dallas. The definition of a plantation at the time was "land planted, often with trees for the purpose of lumbering."

LUCINDA HOAR AND TIMOTHY TIBBETTS. Hoar is believed to be the first white child born (1818) in the lake settlement that was to eventually be known as Rangeley. Her father, Luther, was responsible for the first substantial settlement on Aquassuc Lake. In 1836, Hoar married Timothy Tibbetts. They lived on a farm just three miles from the place of Hoar's birth. They would become parents and grandparents of a very large family that was to be influential in the growth of the community. Descendants became boatbuilders, wheelwrights, and hardware store proprietors. At the time of this 1896 photograph, they celebrated their 60th wedding anniversary. They had 10 children, 49 grandchildren, and 30 great-grandchildren. After this photograph was taken, Hoar lived for seven more years, and Tibbetts lived for another nine years.

SQUIRE RANGELEY. The Rangeley family, Squire James Jr., his wife, Mary, sons John and James, and daughters Sarah, Mary, and Hannah, arrived in 1825 at the settlement that was to bear their name. The squire found the families of Hoar, Dill, Toothaker, Quimby, and Rowe, who had become well-established squatters, living on land he inherited from his father's interest. He resolved potential conflict by selling the families the land for 50¢ per acre and their assistance in building a home for the Rangeleys. The new home, or manor, was located on the hillside overlooking the lake. It had 12 rooms, was one and a half stories high and had a long porch affording a view of the lake. The squire provided for the needs of this small farming community that lacked a village. In 1833, he built dams on two streams, built a gristmill, and then built a shingle mill. This eliminated the farmer's need to haul grain 26 miles down the valley and return with flour. The term "squire" was used to imply prosperity. Soon, more families arrived at the little community with marriages joining them with the original families.

MARY RANGELEY. The squire and his wife, Mary, were greatly saddened by the death of their daughter Sarah, on Christmas day, at age 19. Her death and the remoteness of the region, with its lack of trained medical help, is said to have eventually led the family to leave the community they were responsible for developing. They moved to Phillips in 1841 and then to Portland, before the squire finally settled in Virginia. He died there in 1860. Mary had died five years earlier. Both are buried there. Squire Rangeley left behind a thriving township with dams for mills to process grains and a new road that facilitated movement and commerce. The contributions of the squire have led to him to be considered with a sort of reverence and kindness, as a founding father should be.

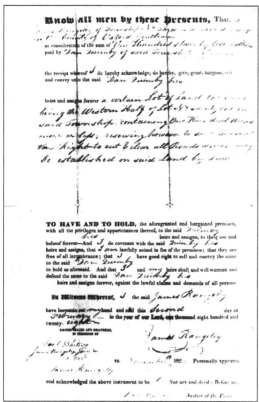

THE DANIEL QUIMBY DEED. In the early 1800s, Dan Quimby, the head of perhaps the second most important family of pioneers, arrived in Rangeley. In 1829, he married Abigail Toothaker and moved into a new farmhouse built on 100 acres of land deeded to him by Squire Rangeley in exchange for digging his 42-foot well. Shown here is one of only three known examples of his signature.

RANGELEY VILLAGE. In 1860, the village of Rangeley was basically a substantial and growing farming community, numbering about 60 persons. The village was located where it is today, on the north side of the lake, just beyond Greenvale Cove, with outlying farms extending around the northern and southeast shores of the lake.

14

FARMING. The early settlement initially relied on farming as the economic basis for the community. Shown here is a farming family haying on the hillside overlooking the lake. Grain, potatoes, apples, and hay were some of the major crops used to feed the farmers and their livestock of cows, horses, and sheep.

A QUIMBY POND BEAN SUPPER. As the town of Rangeley expanded, families continued to identify with their local communities. Quimby Pond, located between Rangeley and the village of Oquossoc, was one such place. Pictured at this community bean supper are members of the families of Rowe, Quimby, Ross, Ellis, Wilbur, Pillsbury, and Edgecomb and a number of unidentified people.

15

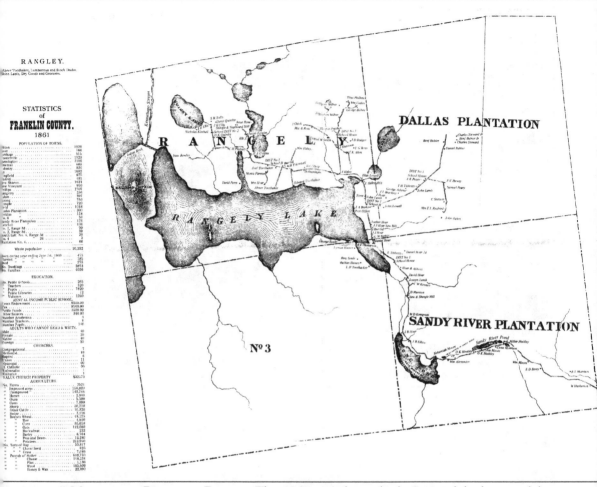

A Map of the Rangeley Region. This 1861 map shows the location of the homes of the early families, including the Bubiers and Oakes, who settled in the area known as Lower and Upper Dallas, and the families of Ellis, Ross, Collins, Wilber, Kimball, Haley, Burnhan, Philbrick, Lamb, Brackett, Steward, Hinkley, Soule, and Haines. Many of their sons left to join the Union forces during the Civil War and never returned due to casualties or the attraction of warmer southern climates. Some chose to head north to avoid conscription. Arriving on the shores of Kennebago Lake, the "skeddalers," or reluctant conscripts, traded furs for supplies. The location still bears the name Skeddaler's Cove.

114 yrs ago

Rangeley Apr 26th 1865 —

Dear Brother and Sister
it is with pleasure that I
Seat My Self to ans your
Latter which I Received Last
Night I was Surprised to hear
that you thought that it was Ally
girl it was all done through a
Mistake I Calculated to tell you
I thought I did tell you it was
Johns Sister I am very Sory
to think had I made Such a
Mistak I was felt So bad that
i did not know what to do
we did not know what to think
because you did not rite but was
dredfull Glad to hear that your Boy
was gitting better I hope that he will
be So that you can Come up here
before long I live to home now

PRESIDENT LINCOLN'S ASSASSINATION. In this letter from Susan Wilber to her brother and sister on April 26, 1865, Wilber writes, "We heard the assassination of President Lincoln and about Secretary Seward. All the particulars in our paper. I hope they catch the villain and give him what he deserves, but I am afraid they won't catch them." She goes on to state, "We hadn't heard from Rufus since the fall of Richmond. We have hunted the paper, but can't hear anything from him and we all going to wait till the next mail and if we hear from him I will write as soon as I get it." Wilber concludes the letter on a positive note, "We had a letter from Rufus. He was well. He has been in all battles and hasn't got a scar. He thinks he will be home in July."

A DAM AT THE OUTLET OF RANGELEY LAKE. In 1833, the squire built two dams to meet the needs of the growing farming community. A shingle and clapboard mill was located at the outlet of Oquossoc (Rangeley) Lake. The mill featured an up-and-down saw. Shown here is the dam as it appeared in 1875.

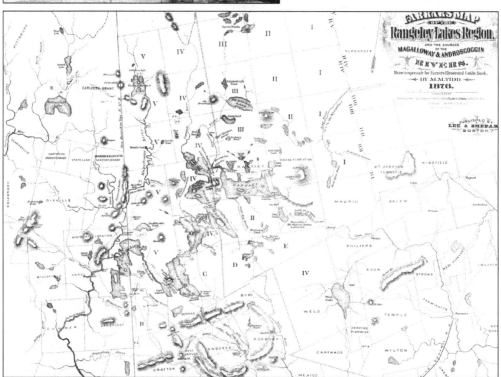

THE RANGELEY LAKES REGION, 1876. Charles Farrar published an 1876 guide book featuring this map of the region. Note the American Indian names for the region's lakes: Mooselookmeguntic (where the hunters watch moose by night), Molechunkamunk (crooked water), Cupsuptic (hemmed in by rocks), Welokenebacook (red water), Kennebago (sweet water), and Umbagog (shallow water). The original name of Aquassuc meant "landing place."

Two

Trophy Brook Trout and Salmon, Guides, and Hunting

A Catch of Trout. In the late 1800s, it was not uncommon to make catches of wild brook trout like the one shown here. Trout were abundant and came readily to the fly or lure. Seen are, from left to right, Fremon E. Timberlake, a businessman; Mellie G. Timberlake; Clarence Hinkley, a guide; and Jess Ross, a guide. Soon, large unregulated catches brought the inevitable decline in the numbers and size of fish.

VOL. XIII   FEBRUARY, 1877   No. 4

SCRIBNER'S MONTHLY. When *Scribner's Monthly* published in 1877 the article "Trout Fishing in the Rangeley Lakes," sportsmen from all over the East Coast headed for Rangeley. The author of the article extolled the virtues of the region and its huge "speckled brook trout."

A TROUT ENGRAVING IN SCRIBNER'S MONTHLY. An engraving of an eight-and-a-half-pound trout caught in 1869 by R. G. Allerton was made from an original drawing of the fish and published as part of the article. Typical of the times, the article related the author's many fishing experiences as he journeyed through the region, with specific directions on how the reader could reach the Rangeley region.

MATCHING A SEVEN-POUND TROUT. This scene from *Scribner's Monthly* illustrates George Shepard Page landing a seven-pound trout after a one-and-a-half-hour battle that extended into the night. The two other boats assisted by surrounding the big fish and providing the light to bring the trout to net.

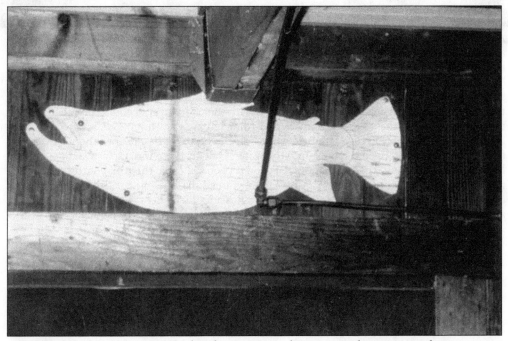

A BIRCH CUTOUT. An economical and convenient alternative to having a taxidermist mount a trophy fish was to trace its outline on a board or piece of birch, cut it out, and tack it on the camp wall. This example is of a $10^{1}/_{2}$-pound trout caught by Elmer Woodbury on July 29, 1904. It was provided by Archer Poor of Upper Dam.

AN 11-POUND 2-OUNCE BROOK TROUT. This trophy trout was caught off the steamer wharf at Bemis by Romey Spaulding, a one-armed fisherman, in the early 1900s and was mounted by Nash of Maine. In the *Phillips Phonograph*, Cornelia "Fly Rod" Crosby recounted the story: "E. J. Spaulding, who for several years and been in Capt. Barker's employ, having charge of the store, was most unfortunate years ago and lost his right arm. . . . All the fishing tackle about the place was in use, except one old rod and reel with some forty feet of cotton line that no one thought of using. Business was dull and Mr. Spaulding having a few minutes of leisure, took this old rod, and putting some nice fat angle worms on the hook, went out onto the wharf, a few feet from the store, dropped the hook into the water. Quickly there was a splash and a fight, for Mr. Trout had yielded to the temptation of a good supper. Off came the reel, but the one armed fisherman finally held the rod between his knees, grasped the line in his left hand and pulled, holding it with his teeth, taking a new hold as fast as a foot or two of the line was brought in, as the fish came up onto the wharf, flopping and jumping."

ANOTHER 11-POUND 2-OUNCE TROUT. This huge fish was caught by an unidentified fisherman at Upper Dam on September 28, 1880, and is believed to be one on the six largest brook trout ever recorded as being caught in Maine. Until 1914, the Rangeley Lake region held the world record for the largest brook trout, which weighed an amazing 12^1/$_2$ pounds.

HUGE BROOK TROUT. It was the huge brook trout that attracted sportsmen from all over the East Coast to the region. These two trout, one seven pounds and the other six pounds, were caught by J. Alger Jr. The huge Rangeley trout were discovered in the 1860s by a group of sportsmen led by Henry O. Stanley, who was to become commissioner of fisheries for the state.

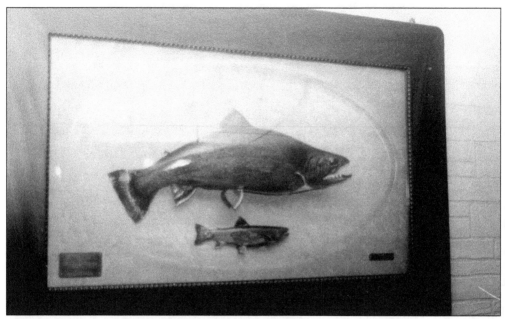

CARRIE STEVENS'S 6-POUND 13-OUNCE BROOK TROUT. This fish, caught by Carrie Stevens in 1924, won her second place in a *Field & Stream* magazine contest. The publicity she received for catching this prize on a fly of her own design resulted in a flood of orders for her flies, and thus she began a career as one of the country's most famous fly tiers.

PLEASANT ISLAND TROUT. Pleasant Island is situated in Cupsuptic Lake and was the site of many catches of large brook trout. The unidentified guide and sportsmen appear to be pleased with this catch of a trout that could be in the neighborhood of 10 pounds.

MOOSELOOKMEGUNTIC TROUT.
Shown here is Mr. Simpson,
posing with his six-and-a-half-
pound brook trout taken from
Mooselookmeguntic Lake.

THE LADIES' CATCH. Here is a nice catch by two unidentified ladies fishing on
Mooselookmeguntic Lake in 1886. Note the more formal dress that was common even while
fishing in the northern woods of Maine.

A BALD MOUNTAIN CAMPS CATCH. This photograph shows five unidentified men on the porch of their camp at Bald Mountain Camps during the late 1890s with their catch of trout and salmon hanging from twig rings. The unidentified woman (second from the left) is probably Cornelia "Fly Rod" Crosby, who often stayed at these camps.

AN INCREDIBLE CATCH OF TROUT. This string of 23 trout weighed a total of 104³/4 pounds and was taken by fishermen at the Oquossoc Angling Association. Many members of the OAA released most of the day's catch. They towed fish cars (wooden boxes with holes to allow water to flow through) to keep their catch alive. They transferred the trout to bigger containers and took home only the largest fish, releasing the remainder.

Oquassa trout; blueback trout; quasky, *Salvelinus oquassa* (Girard). Breeding female, 15 inches long. From Rangeley Stream, Oquossoc, Me.

A BLUEBACK TROUT. Many people feel that the much smaller blueback trout was the reason that the Rangeley region brook trout reached such mammoth size. These less colorful members of the char family provided an abundant source of forage for the brook trout. They were October spawners that came into the small streams at night in tremendous numbers. Locals using dip nets filled barrels with the small trout for their winter provisions. The tasty bluebacks were shipped throughout Maine and even to the Fulton Fish Market in New York City. Excess fishing pressure and the introduction of landlocked salmon led to their disappearance in the early 1900s. This corresponded to the decline in the number and size of the fabled brook trout. Smelt were introduced into the region's waters c. 1877 to supplement the declining numbers of bluebacks. The smelt thrived in the cold waters and also provided an opportunity for local residents to take up a new form of spring recreation, smelting.

THE OQUOSSOC FISH HATCHERY. The first fish hatchery in the region, on Bemis Stream, was established by George Shephard Page, L. Crounse, and H. Hutchinson, members of the Oquossoc Angling Association. In 1875, it produced 250,000 trout for stocking in local waters. In the 1880s, another hatchery was opened in Oquossoc on the Rangeley River by the OAA. It has recently been commercially raising salmon that are then taken to pens on the Maine coast to reach market size.

Landlocked salmon, *Salmo sebago* (Girard). Breeding male, 19 inches long. From Rangeley Stream, Oquossoc, Me.

LANDLOCKED SALMON. In an effort to supplement the declining population of brook trout, members of the OAA introduced another species, the landlocked salmon, known for its fighting ability and acrobatics. It took a while before the salmon acclimated to the local waters, but soon they were being caught in significant numbers at trophy size.

28

A TROPHY SALMON.
A. C. Lawrence is shown holding his eight-and-a-quarter-pound salmon in this late-1800s view. His guide was S. B. McCard. Note the Rangeley boat on the dock behind him.

ANOTHER TROPHY SALMON. A group of unidentified sportsmen and their guide are shown in front Noble Cottage in the late 1800s. The salmon appears to be about 10 pounds or even more.

A RECORD RANGELEY LANDLOCKED SALMON. This huge salmon, held by two unidentified boys and a man in front of the Mountain View House in 1931, is reported to have been 30 inches long and 12 inches deep. The weight is estimated at 22 pounds; although that seems questionable, it is still a trophy.

RANGELEY LAKES REGION GUIDES. The Maine guide, with his knapsack, is shown pointing the way in this brochure published by the Maine Central and Sandy River Railroads. The advertising piece promotes the region's plentiful fishing and hunting opportunities. In 1910, there were 120 guides serving the region. In 1900, the *New England Magazine* praised the Rangeley guides as "a fine stalwart set of men."

Twenty years life in Rangeley

It is our intention to tell nothing
but the truth and not all of that
I get some from old Guides and
trapers but the bigest part I am knowing
to myself

     I was born in Havenhill N. H
I maried a Maine girl the daughter of
Old Dady S Clarke one of the oldest
Guides about the Lakes We came here fr
Franconia N H the spring of 1871 it
was good wheling when we left It We came
from Farmington to Phillips with Unkle
John Pickens on the old stage we stoped
over night at the Barden House in the morni
we came in to Wm Huleys with Moses Well
on a sleigh we stoped there a spell Then
moved into a little house at the foot of

A GUIDE'S DIARY. A recently discovered handwritten diary of an unidentified guide begins, "It is our intention to tell nothing but the truth and not all of that. I get some from old guides and trappers, but the biggest part I am knowing to myself. I was born in Havenhill N.H. I married a Maine girl, the daughter of old Daddy S. Clarke, one of the oldest guides about the lakes. We came here from Franconia N.H. the spring of 1871." Subsequent research determined that the diary was written by Cal Pennock, who portrays life as a guide in the 1870s. This honest and humorous account talks about the sports he guided, their catches, camp life, and how they managed during the long, cold winter. Pennock went on to write an outdoor column for an area newspaper.

THE RANGELEY LAKES GUIDE'S ASSOCIATION. On November 7, 1896, the Rangeley Lakes Guide's Association was formed "to protect and aid the propagation of fish and game, to secure wise and practical legislation, to secure good reliable guides and to regulate a uniform rate of wages." It is also reported they were strongly opposed to Cornelia "Fly Rod" Crosby's effort to license guides. Today, the association includes sportsmen and has over 600 members.

A GUIDE'S CAMP. A guide's role was not only to locate fish or game for the sport but also to provide transportation, shelter, and good food. Often, the measure of a guide was strongly influenced by the quality of his cooking.

JOHN JAY WILBUR. In the early 1900s, guiding was a major economic occupation in the Rangeley region. John Jay Wilbur was one of those early guides. Shown here in front of the old Rangeley post office, Wilbur was guide to the Whitney family. Often times, a family or individual would hire a favorite guide for the season and continue the relationship for many years.

MAINE DEER. Whitetail deer could be found in any of the New England states, but nowhere did the deer grow to the huge size that they did in Maine. Deer weighing 200 pounds or over with huge racks of 10, 12, and more points attracted sportsmen from throughout the East Coast. They journeyed to the Rangeley region, staying in rough camps in hopes of bringing home that trophy.

ROUGH CAMP. Accommodations at hunting camps were limited; they were simply a place to sleep, prepare a hot meal, and tell stories of the day's adventure. These unidentified men appear to be relaxing while one checks his rifle.

SEVEN SPORTS AT REST. At Billy Soule's camps on Cupsuptic Lake, seven unidentified sports pose in their best hunting and fishing attire. Note the combination of fly fishing rods, nets, and guns.

Two Deer. Shown in the center of this photograph of two deer and two hunters is Sid Harden, the local game warden and historian. Harden equipped his familiar truck like a traveling camp, with a bed, stove, heater, lights, and other comforts of home.

Moose. Moose and caribou were much sought after by early sportsmen, but their numbers were soon depleted. It was not until recent years that wildlife management practices and the clear-cutting of large tracks of woodland provided adequate browse for the expansion of the moose herd and introduction of a permitted hunting season.

HUNTING AND TRAPPING CAMPS. This is a typical winter camp used by trappers in the valley of the Upper Magalloway north of Parmachenee Lake. In their book *Hunting and Trapping*, Fred Barker and John Danforth recounted their 1876–1877 trapping adventures in this area.

TRAPPING. Beaver abound in the Rangeley region and have long afforded an opportunity for residents to supplement their income during the winter months. Shown here is Skeet Davenport, a master guide, holding a beaver skin being tagged by Jack Show, the warden supervisor, on the left and Ray Ellis, a warden, in the middle.

Three

GETTING THERE, GETTING AROUND

ROUGH ROADS TO RANGELEY. The high mountains, a series of lakes, and an impenetrable forest of fir, spruce, maple, and birch challenged the first visitors to the region. However, they used old American Indian trails that followed well-traveled game trails across the mountains and along river valleys to reach the area called Ammerascaegin (Androscoggin). Gradually, rough roads replaced the trails, but travel was slow and often dangerous.

MUD SEASON. Spring thaws turned frozen roads to deep mud, making travel difficult if not impossible. This buckboard driver, en route from Loon Lake to Kennebago Lake, discovered just how arduous travel was during the appropriately named mud season. Often, winter travel was done on ice, but as it thawed, it was a necessary to use the muddy roads even if it meant getting stuck, which was preferable to getting wet.

BUCKBOARD TRAVEL. This group of unidentified partygoers is seen in a Starbird photograph as they venture forth over rough roads.

THE STEAMER UNION. When sportsmen arrived in the region, they used the many lakes to reach their final destinations. Shown here is the first of a long line of steamers that plied the lakes. The *Union* was the pioneer steamer and not much more than a old scow with a wheel behind and an upright boiler and engine.

Excursion on the Rangeley Lake

THE STEAMER RANGELEY. Leaving the terminus at the foot of Lake Street in the city, the steamer *Rangeley* brought visitors to the hotels and camps located around the lake and connections with steamers on adjacent waters. Excursions of upwards of 100 people were also popular.

CAPTAIN SOULE. The steamer *Rangeley* was captained by H. Soule, aided by engineer C. Hamblin. Also shown is passenger M. Schmidt. The steamers transported passengers to their destinations or excursions on the lake.

THE STEAMER *FLORENCE BARKER*. Named for the captain's daughter, the *Florence Barker* was one of many steamers owned by the captain. It served his camps on Mooselookmeguntic and connected travelers with Haines Landing and Upper Dam.

THE DEMISE OF THE STEAMER RANGELEY. This 1890s photograph shows the steamer *Rangeley* after it was burned. Also in the photograph is Rangeley's first hand pumper fire wagon. Most steamers met a similar fate as they aged or the competition from automobiles made their services no longer economical.

THE SANDY RIVER AND RANGELEY LAKES RAILROAD. The railroad was extended to Rangeley from Phillips on July 1, 1891. Known as the narrow gauge, or two-footer, it consisted of 3 locomotives, 3 passenger cars, 5 boxcars, 5 service cars, and 35 flatcars. Obviously, the primary focus of the narrow gauge was lumbering.

TRAINS IN THE WINTER. The heavy snows in the Western Mountains of Maine made railroad travel challenging for passengers and crew. Outfitted with a snowplow, the trains were used to keep the tracks clear.

A WINTER TRAIN WRECK. It was not uncommon on the narrow-gauge Sandy River and Rangeley Lakes Railroad to experience a derailment of an engine or, occasionally, the entire train due to the track displacement by snow, ice, or debris. The small engine size permitted jacks, chains, crowbars, and a second engine to soon have it upright.

A 1906 TRAIN WRECK. Train derailments occurred due to sharp grades and curves, even when weather was not a factor. Shown here is a derailment of the entire train on September 8, 1906, on Cook's Grade, just north of nearby Strong.

THE LAST RUN TO RANGELEY. This photograph shows one of the last runs of the narrow gauge to Rangeley in the early 1930s. The railroads succumbed to competition from motorcars and trucks. This car was converted to a wide gauge and used between Oquossoc and Kennebago.

THE OQUOSSOC RAIL STATION. The Rumford Falls and Rangeley Lakes Railroad was extended from Bemis to the community of Oquossoc in 1902; thus the region was served by two separate railroads. This scene is of the standard gauge arriving in Oquossoc to be met by horse-drawn carriages from nearby hotels to transport guests to their lodgings. The rail line was later extended to Kennebago Lake.

A RANGELEY BOAT. The boats used to take sports to the fishing grounds needed to be durable and easy to row. Members of the OAA selected a boat from Ogdensburg, New York, to pattern their own version after. Its design was canoe-like with a sharp stern. Its strength came from the lapped strakes of cedar and the many half-round ribs lining the inside. Important builders include Tibbetts, Tufts, Loomis, Barrett, Collins, and Ellis.

A Snow Machine. Winter travel provided many challenges that led to innovation. In 1915, Ed Lowell, a game warden, built one of the first snowmobiles using an early Ford that was modified with a pair of skis and rear tracts to propel the snow machine over snow depths of five to six feet.

Dog Sled Mail Delivery. Fred Fowler delivered mail to Upper Dam (shown here) and to Grant's Camps at Kennebago during the 1930s. Fowler, a trapper, woodsman, and sporting store operator, ran the only dogsled mail delivery in the eastern United States. His team consisted of between 5 and 11 Baffin Land and Labrador huskies, depending on the load to be carried.

THE BLACK CAT CAMP, C. 1890. Logging began soon after European American settlers arrived. In 1833, James Rangeley Jr. built a shingle mill on Rangeley Lake. Coe and Pingree erected the Upper and Middle Dams on Mooselookmeguntic Lake for log drives 20 years later. When this crew lined up at John R. Toothaker's Black Cat Camp, lumbering prospered. Toothaker (far left) had a newly married son, Lincoln (fourth from the left), who served as camp clerk and drove a team of gray Percherons, Dick and Phil. "Link" rose at 4:00 a.m. to tend the horses and refused to leave them in anyone else's care until an 1892 accident led to his departure and the amputation of his leg. Loggers cut spruce from October to spring, from sunup until dusk, Monday through Saturday. Sundays brought visits from snowshoeing family and friends. In letters to his wife, Idella, Link complained of molasses and beans for every meal and hot tea "strong enough to kill a hog." What little meat they had was venison. The camp charged extra for liver. Also pictured are Charles Toothaker, Allon Wilbur, men of the Haley and Haines families, and others. (Courtesy of Becky Ellis Martineau.)

Four

LOGGING THE TIMBERWOODS

THE HEAD WORKS AT OQUOSSOC, 1906. With capstan, head works, bateau, and anchor, loggers boomed logs across Rangeley Lake, cut the booms (necklace-like strings of logs that held logs together), and sluiced the logs through the dam. They floated the logs down Rangeley River into Mooselookmeguntic Lake and boomed them to Bemis, where they were sawed, loaded into train cars, and shipped to Rumford. (Courtesy of the Will Otis Collection, Maine Forest and Logging Museum.)

RIVER DRIVERS, 1906. Pickpoles in hand, river drivers, including Will Otis (sixth from the left), prepare to sluice, or guide, logs through the dam's sluiceway near Oquossoc and into Rangeley River. Oquossoc became a lively place, with the Dead Rat boardinghouse, whose owner drove into the woods to pick up loggers. Vance Oakes assured folklorist Edward Ives, "I'm telling you, boy, they'd wake up in the morning without a nickel." (Courtesy of the Will Otis Collection, Maine Forest and Logging Museum.)

DYNAMITE! Logjams on Rangeley River were hazardous. Peaveys in their hands and spiked boots on their feet, men would pull out several key logs and run back before the jam gave way. Sometimes, loggers would have to use dynamite. Loggers, such as Gaylon "Jeep" Wilcox, who worked on the Dead River, nearly died when jams gave way before they could jump ashore. (Courtesy of the Will Otis Collection, Maine Forest and Logging Museum.)

Late 1950's DALLAS PLT,
by Walter Manchester
Mechanic Falls Me.

BULLDOZING PULPWOOD, THE 1950S. River drives in the 20th century on the South Branch of the Dead River employed many Rangeley men, such as Rodney Richard Sr., Ernest Morin, and Delbert Green. These men, with bulldozers, trucks, and, later, cranes, pushed pulpwood into the water. Morin also served as Hudson Pulp and Paper's scaler for many years, measuring the wood that loggers cut. Here, a bulldozer driver readies wood for a drive. (Courtesy of the Dead River Historical Society.)

A DEAD RIVER DRIVE, 1948. During the drives, pulp filled the Dead River, shown here from behind Leavitt's store in Flagstaff Village. Crews followed the wood down from Dallas Landing through Fansanger Falls, across Flagstaff Lake, through the sluice at Long Falls Dam (after 1950), through Dead River Dam and Dead River Rapids, and onto the Forks, where the Dead River joins the Kennebec for the trip to the mills and Augusta. (Courtesy of Clarence Jones.)

TAKING THE REAR, 1969. Ralph Roy (left), Willy Kakhonen, Mell Targett, and Clarence Jones take the rear, freeing wood that got hung up during a drive on the Dead River's South Branch. On July 24, 1972, the last drive began at Hayden Landing, below Dead River Dam. Loggers, such as Glen Viles of North Anson, drove 7,108 cords of wood, a smaller amount than usual, to Scott Paper in Winslow. (Photograph by Brad Crafts, courtesy of Clarence Jones.)

HANDLING BATEAUX, 1954. To many loggers, Clarence Jones's skills handling bateaux are legendary. "Clarence was quick as a cat," remembers Richard Morin. Jones worked the full length of the Dead River drives from 1938 to 1964, as well as parts of the Dead River and other drives such as this one on Big Spencer Stream. Seen are Clarence Jones (left, in the stern); Erwin Targett Jr.; Kenneth Packard; and Jerry White, the bow man. (Courtesy of Clarence Jones.)

TIMBER SPRUCE, C. 1935. On Long Pond's road, built by the Civilian Conservation Corps, Leon Oakes (left) and Bart Morton bind two-foot-wide old-growth timber spruce logs and their homemade pole trailer with chains before heading to Kempton Lumber in Archie Carignan's International truck. Before loggers had mechanical equipment, they built yards (left) and rolled logs on trailers using hand tools such as peaveys. (Courtesy of the Ben Morton Collection, the Rangeley Lakes Region Logging Museum.)

DELIVERING LOGS, C. 1935. At Kempton Lumber Company, Bart Morton (left) and Leon Oakes get ready to roll spruce logs off Archie Carignan's International truck and into a boom on Rangeley Lake, where an endless chain carried the logs into the building. The mill burned sawdust to generate steam for the engines, and children such as Ronnie Haines played in the towering sawdust piles outside. The Rangeley Lake House is in the background. (Courtesy of the Ben Morton Collection, the Rangeley Lakes Region Logging Museum.)

KEMPTON LUMBER, C. 1920. One of several mills, Rangeley's Kempton Lumber stood at the west end of town. Here, Riley Hinkley loads lumber onto a wagon. When the buildings burned in 1939, townspeople gathered to watch. Kempton rebuilt. About 20 years later, Bart Morton cleared the site with his big crane for Carl Davis's marina that opened in 1961. Local people purchased the mill's large timbers. (Rangeley Lakes Region Historical Society.)

THE KEMPTON CREW, 1920. Kempton Lumber provided Rangeley with work, as this photograph of part of the crew shows. Seen here are, from left to right, the following: (first row) Charles Hardy; (second row) Roy Dunham and Harry Hawkurst; (third row) Fern Toothaker and Leslie Doak; (fourth row) Guy Bean, George Kempton, and Erlon Jones; (fifth row) Lowell Lawrence, Blanch Tomlinson, Lyman Kempton, and Alman Wilbur. (Rangeley Lakes Region Historical Society.)

RANGELEY TRUCKS, DECEMBER 1938. Ben Morton and Eddie West hand-loaded pulpwood cut by Stratton Road farmers into Ed Myshrall's single-axle Chevrolet trucks and drove to the International Paper mill in Livermore Falls. In 25-below-zero weather, they put canvas in front of the radiators to keep them from pulling in cold air. Under his leather mittens, Ben wore wool ones that his mother, Annie, knitted. Tight wrists kept the snow out. (Courtesy of the Ben Morton Collection, the Rangeley Lakes Region Logging Museum.)

MILL BROOK, 1949. Elijah White (right rear) hauled crew, including Ralph Virgin (front), and equipment by power company barge to Mill Brook on Upper Richardson Lake, cutting 45,000 board feet of pine logs a day for Timberlands in Dixfield. On the barge are two D4 Caterpillar crawlers as well as No. 1 "Muscles" (right rear), an early skidder that he made from an FWD snowplow. (Courtesy of the White Collection, the Rangeley Lakes Region Logging Museum.)

CATCHING KEY LOGS, 1943. From 1942 to 1943, the U.S. Office of War Information assigned photographers to document war production throughout the country. John Collier Jr. (1913–1992) traveled to the Brown Company's timberlands and recorded the spring 1943 drive. Feeding pulpwood through the sluice at Long Pond, north of Kennebago Lake, this woodsman catches a key log with the twisted point of his pickpole. Other logs follow. (Photograph by John Collier Jr., courtesy of the Library of Congress.)

SLUICING AT KENNEBAGO, 1943. The drive kept a southerly course. It streamed down the Kennebago River, got towed down Mooselookmeguntic Lake and Upper and Lower Richardson Lakes, barreled through Rapid River into Umbagog Lake, and traveled the Androscoggin River to the Brown Company mills in Berlin, New Hampshire. Here, woodsmen with pickpoles feed logs into the sluice at the power dam on the Kennebago. (Photograph by John Collier Jr., courtesy of Library of Congress.)

OPENING THE BOOM, 1943. Woodsmen on the drive needed to be catty on their feet, and pickpoles, caulked boots with sharp spikes protruding from their soles, and short, ragged pants legs all helped. At the upper end of Mooselookmeguntic, this logger opens up an empty boom so it can be filled with logs from the Kennebago River. The last boom passed through Upper Dam in 1952. (Photograph by John Collier Jr., courtesy of Library of Congress.)

TOWING A BOOM OF LOGS, 1943. A steamer, probably the *H. P. Frost,* stretches the boom around logs it must tow down Mooselookmeguntic. To tow the boom, the steamer ran ahead a quarter of a mile, cast anchor, and winched the boom toward it. With a fair wind, the *H. P. Frost* made the 12-mile haul in 16 hours. Given strong wind in the wrong direction, the steamer cast anchor to prevent being blown back. (Photograph by John Collier Jr., courtesy of Library of Congress.)

THE TWO O'CLOCK MEAL, 1943.
Woodsmen ate four meals a day
throughout the drive. At 10:00 a.m.
and 2:00 p.m., they ate near their
work, serving themselves cafeteria
style with plenty of second helpings.
Here, their menu includes roast
pork and dressing, boiled potatoes,
turnips, baked beans, hot cakes, hot
biscuits, bread, butter, several kinds
of cookies, gingerbread, doughnuts,
apple and orange pie, milk, tea,
coffee, and water. (Photograph by
John Collier Jr., courtesy of Library
of Congress.)

A BUNKHOUSE, MAY 1943. After a 13-hour day driving logs and pulpwood, woodsmen relax in
the Brown Company bunkhouse during the evening, playing cards, greasing their spiked boots,
mending their pants, and listening to the radio, their only direct link to the outside world. A
generation later, Kennebec river driver David Calder captured the rewards of a woodsman's life
in his song "River Drive." (Photograph by John Collier Jr., courtesy of Library of Congress.)

Five

CAMPS AND HOTELS

THE DEAD RIVER POND CAMPS (SADDLEBACK LAKE CAMPS). These early camps, originally known as Dead River Pond Camps, were located at the foot of the 4,000-foot Saddleback Mountain. Hemon Blackwell operated the camps for fishing in 1912. He sold them to a group of Rhode Island doctors for use as a private fishing camp and for lumber speculation. Monett and Gertrude Robbins purchased the camps in 1935.

SADDLEBACK LAKE LODGE. Monett Robbins started with six log camps and began to expanded his business along with his second wife, Peg. He applied to change the name Dead River Pond to Saddleback Lake. Together, they ran the lodge and numerous log camps until 1971. Monett and Peg were very active in statewide tourism organizations and brought a high degree of professionalism to the lodging business in Rangeley.

THE SADDLEBACK LODGE CAMPS. Perhaps one of the most photographed scenes in Maine was the camp on the point with Saddleback Mountain in the background. This scene was the subject of a mural on the wall of Grand Central Station in New York in the 1930s. Monett Robins told the story of cutting down a tree at the height of autumn color and propping it up on the point to add an interesting touch for an advertisement featuring the famous scene.

58

THE SEVEN PONDS. Ed Grant established the Seven Ponds Camps in 1876 and subsequently expanded to include overnight shelters on ponds in the Seven Ponds region. Note the wood chimneys lined with mud and rocks, which certainly contributed to the risk of fire. To reach the camps from Kennebago Lake, guests had to travel five miles by steamer, two miles upstream by rowboat, one mile across Little Kennebago by rowboat, another two miles upstream by rowboat, and finally six miles across a carry.

GRANT'S KENNEBAGO CAMPS. These camps were started in 1904 by Will and Hall Grant. According to Gary Priest in his book *History of Rangeley Hotels and Camps*, their father, Ed Grant, helped them row boatloads of boards down the lake to build new camps. During the winter of 1912–1913, the camps remained open all winter and had up to 30 guests, mostly railroad and lumbering officials. A fire in 1977 destroyed the main dining room and several camps, but they were rebuilt, and the camps continue in operation today.

CAMP SKENOSUS. This is one of four double outcamps that were connected by a porch on Kennebago Lake. They were built by Ed Grant and the Richardsons for their clients who liked to fish at the lower end of the lake and Kennebago River.

CAMP CROSBY AT KENNEBAGO LAKE. This rough camp located on the shores of Kennebago Lake provided an ideal spot for trout fishing and hunting in the late 1800s. The camp was also occupied by women and children. Included in the picture of mostly unidentified people is Roland York (third from the right), who was to operate his own camps.

60

THE FOREST RETREAT HOUSE. The first camp on Kennebago Lake was built in 1871 by George Snowman and served as a cabin and trading post. By 1877, there were two rough camps that required sportsmen to bring in and cook their own food. In a partnership, Ed Grant purchased the property. Grant sold it to the Richardsons and left to concentrate on his venture at Beaver Pond.

KENNEBAGO
LAKE HOUSE and CAMPS

OFF For A Days Fun
At
KENNEBAGO

Where there is fly fishing
throughout the Season
In the heart of the
North MAINE Woods

AN EARLY KENNEBAGO LAKE HOUSE. In 1909, the Kennebago Hotel Company purchased the Forest Retreat House. For many years, they were operated by Harry Look Sr. Fishing for the famous Kennebago brook trout continued to draw sportsmen to this somewhat remote area. As business increased so did the hotel, and by 1912, there were 13 cabins and a 10-room main camp. Electricity arrived in 1916 and added another convenience to the largest camp on Kennebago.

THE KENNEBAGO LAKE HOUSE. Harry Look Sr. sold his share in 1924 and left to run Pickford Camps on Rangeley Lake. J. Lewis York purchased the camps at auction in 1935 to complement his business at York's Camps. Bud Russell bought out Sam York in 1950 and built a bypass road so guests did not have to pass through York's Lodge. In the early 1970s, the hotel was razed, its contents were auctioned, and the camps sold individually.

YORK'S CAMPS. Originally known as Forest Camps when built in 1889, the camps were purchased outright by Roland York in 1896, and their name was changed. He served as a cook at the camps, and during the winter, he would hire out as a cook for logging camps. Upon his death in 1902, his son J. Lewis took over York's Camps at age 20. The camps were well known for the huge fireplace, trophy mounts, and rustic furnishings. The camps remained in the family until they closed.

SAGAMORE LODGE. Located on Quimby Pond, this lodge was built by Sam Hano as a private camp. The lodge originally consisted of six interconnected log buildings set side by side. A unique feature of these buildings is the round ceilings that remind people of the bottom of a canoe. A piazza extends the more than 100-foot length of the lodge along the shore of Quimby Pond. The trophy room contains over 60 mounts of fish, deer, moose, caribou, elk, and birds. After passing through the hands of several owners, the Hano Camp was purchased by Phil Perry and Howard Herrick, who opened it to the public in 1927 as Sagamore Lodge. Additional outlying camps were added, bringing the total to 11. At the height of operations, the lodge and camps could accommodate 40 guests. Sagamore has been completely restored to its 1930s appearance and is now a private residence.

*Mountain View House
Oquossoc Maine
about 1875*

AN EARLY MOUNTAIN VIEW HOUSE. George Soule built a camp at the outlet of Rangeley Lake called Camp Henry. It was probably leased by Henry T. Kimball in 1878, when a larger, less rustic building was constructed on the same site. Reflecting the seasonal growth of the area, it was opened as a hotel with 20 sleeping rooms. In 1894, John and Rosie Toothaker sold the Mountain View House to Henry Kimball.

THE MOUNTAIN VIEW HOUSE. In 1895, the building was expanded with an annex whose fireplace could accommodate five-foot logs. It advertised a billiard parlor, lawn tennis, croquet, and archery. By 1900, the hotel could accommodate 85 guests. The property changed hands several times and closed during World War II. The main building was razed, and the annex was converted to a dining room and cocktail lounge. It was subdivided and sold as individual lots in 1959.

64

THE MINGO SPRINGS HOTEL. Two camps were built in 1896 that were to eventually become the Mingo Springs Hotel. A new dining room was added in 1900. The large hotel shown here was built in 1906. The name was soon changed to Mingo Springs. New camps, tennis courts, and a golf course were added over the next several years. In 1965, the hotel furnishings were auctioned, the hotel was torn down, and the cottages were sold individually.

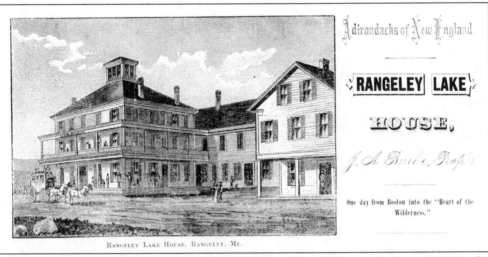

THE RANGELEY LAKE HOUSE. The Lake House was built by John A. Burke in 1876 on the Main Street site of the first private hotel, which was destroyed in the Great Fire of 1876. Often referred to as Hinkley's Hotel, it became the leading hotel in the city, serving sportsmen and their families for 19 years. In 1895–1896, it was moved in two sections to the lakeshore. In this advertising brochure, it referred to Rangeley as "the Adirondacks of New England, one day from Boston in the heart of the wilderness."

THE RANGELEY LAKE HOUSE, THE 20TH CENTURY. Demand for greater comfort and amenities led to the creation of a 20-room, four-story annex, an enlarged kitchen, and a furnace to heat the kitchen and dining room. The enhanced Lake House is shown *c.* 1916 with its emphasis on golfing, luxury accommodations, fine dining, beautiful gardens, evening parties, boating, bathing, a water carnival, tennis, baseball, "autoing," pool, croquet, and bridge. The evening parties were described as follows: "In the evening, the younger set is ready for the dancing parties or private theatricals in the Casino to close the day's festivities. The Casino is just far enough

away from the hotel so that those who prefer a quiet chat or rubber of bridge on the verandas or in the sun parlor are not disturbed." In a short span of 50 years, the accommodations had changed dramatically from primitive to luxurious. Golfing was encouraged: "To drive from the tee directly in front of the main hotel entrance and the fields in the clear Rangeley air gives one a splendid appetite, stirs the blood, clears the brain and builds up the muscles." Oh yes, fishing was still popular.

GOLFING AT THE LAKE HOUSE. Golfing was a popular leisure pastime. Shown here are two men identified only as Ralph and Tom. The man on the left was a one-armed golf pro at the Rangeley Lake House in the mid-1920s.

THE RANGELEY LAKE HOUSE INTERIOR. A sense of the hotel's elegance can be seen in this interior photograph of the Lake House. Seen are a piano in the corner, gaslights, and comfortable rocking chairs, one of which still survives today in the Rangeley Lakes Region Historical Society. Residents of the town always knew when the hotel's elevator was in use because their lights would dim.

THE RANGELEY LAKE HOUSE BOARDWALK. Access to the city was a pleasant walk along the lake on the boardwalk. A stroll into the city brought you to many fine shops, including a millinery, clothing store, pharmacy, and, importantly, a theater that played many first-run motion pictures. It was said that guests in this remote part of Maine often saw the latest Charlie Chaplin silent film before their friends back home in Boston, New York, or Philadelphia.

THE RANGELEY LAKE HOUSE DEMISE. The Lake House remained a major part of the community until social changes brought about after World War II caused its demise in the late 1950s. The building was demolished, the furnishings were auctioned off, and the property was subdivided, thus bringing an end to the great hotel era.

DOCTOR'S ISLAND. Frederick Dickson purchased the island for his wife as a compromise between his desire to be near his favorite fishing at Kennebago and her desire for a less isolated location. Many terraced gardens were added over the years, making it a showplace for the many guest of the Dicksons. Fire destroyed the house in 1939. After World War II, it was opened with eight housekeeping camps. Today, it is a private residence.

PICKFORD'S CAMPS. Built by Henry and Sherman Pickford in 1898, the main lodge consisted of a large dining room, main office, and ladies reception room together with four log camps. Harry Look Sr. took over the management for the Kennebago Hotel Company in 1916. During the winters, Look managed the Rangeley Tavern. The Pickford camp's contents and buildings were auctioned in 1975, and the remaining property was sold off in individual lots.

PLEASANT ISLAND CAMPS. Billy Soule's camps, located on Pleasant Island on Cupsuptic Lake, were described in *Glimpses of New England:* "The ten fine sporting Camps are unique in architecture, rustic in finish, and luxurious in furnishings, with an elaborate cuisine and service second to no sporting camp in Maine. Trophies of game and fish decorate the office and rooms of the camps."

THE EARLY OQUOSSOC ANGLING ASSOCIATION. At Indian Rock, Perley Smith sold his camps to Cornelius Richardson in the 1860s. The Oquossoc Angling Association was formed in 1868 and purchased the camps. Camp Kennebago was built in 1869. The main building contained three apartments, a kitchen, a dining room, and a general sitting room and bedroom. A women's building was added in 1878. An Indian Rock post office was also established.

THE OQUOSSOC ANGLING ASSOCIATION INTERIOR. Many stories of trophy trout were told around this huge fireplace in the main camp at OAA. Five-foot logs provided a warmth from the chill of the spring and fall evenings. The private camp remains much the same today as it appeared in the early 1900s.

THE OQUOSSOC ANGLING ASSOCIATION. The association's purpose was to preserve and protect the exceptional brook trout fishery. To replenish the numbers of trout, members built and operated a hatchery and breeding ponds on Bema (Bemis) Stream. The OAA was also instrumental in introducing landlocked salmon to supplement the dwindling supply of trout and stocking smelt to provide additional forage.

THE MOOSELOOKMEGUNTIC HOUSE. George Soule opened to the public the first building at Haines Landing in 1877. By 1886, it became the Mooselookmeguntic House and consisted of 50 rooms located on two floors with a broad veranda on the lakeside front. Ownership of the hotel changed hands several times as more cabins were added. The hotel burned to the ground in 1958, and the remaining 27 cabins were eventually subdivided and sold as private residences.

BALD MOUNTAIN CAMPS. The camps on the shores of Mooselookmeguntic were opened to the public in 1898, with six camps connected by a long piazza. It was purchased in 1942 by Ronnie and Rose Turmenne from Samuel Eastwood, who had operated the camps since 1923. The much respected camps are one of the few early camps still operating today in the old manner, by the Philbrick family.

LAKEWOOD CAMPS. This camp was originally called Angler's Retreat. The name was changed to Lakewood by Ed Coburn in 1909. Larry and Alys Parsons acquired the camps and added a new hardwood floor in the dining room that was removed from the dance hall at Upper Dam. A 1957 fire destroyed the main lodge and several cabins, which were rebuilt. Now owned and operated by the Carters, Lakewood still accommodates guests for fishing the nearby famed Rapid River.

CAMP BEMIS. The wonderful trout fishing at the lower end of Mooselookmeguntic Lake led members of the Oquossoc Angling Association to build some camps near Bemis Stream prior to 1877. When these early camps were sold to Capt. Fred C. Barker in 1880, he tore them down and erected Camp Bemis. The main dining room was appropriately named Cleft Rock Hall after the split rock located in the front.

74

CAMP BEMIS EXPANDED. By 1884, Captain Barker added nine log cabins and a six-room framed house, and the camps could accommodate 30 guests. Early access to the camps was by steamers run by Captain Barker. The railroad arrived from Rumford in 1897, further expanding the number of visitors to Bemis.

THE BIRCHES. Recognizing the business opportunities of catering to the great influx of fishermen, Captain Barker built a set of camps on Student's Island in 1885 on Mooselookmeguntic Lake. Several years later, he changed the name of the camp from Student's Island to the Birches in order to discourage the feeling that they were camps for students. Fire claimed 11 of the 28 camps in 1925. Five of the remaining buildings were hauled over the ice to a new location, the Barker Hotel.

Rangeley Lakes, Me.

THE BARKER HOTEL. In 1902, Captain Barker foresaw the changing taste of the guests at his other camps. He built a 35-room hotel on 1,300 feet of Mooselookmeguntic shore frontage. The main building had a large kitchen that could serve 150 guests, a lighthouse-sized cupola, and a main office. More log camps were added, including the five moved from the Birches. The captain advertised, "Here, remote from all the bustle of the business world, with an elevation

of nearly 2,000 feet above the sea, with an atmosphere dry and invigorating. . . . Hay fever is positively unknown." When Fred died in 1937, his daughter Florence and her husband, Ray Harnden, took over until 1950, when they sold it to their son Fred Harnden. The hotel was closed in 1966 and was demolished; the camps were sold off—an all too familiar end to the hotels of the region.

UPPER DAM. Perhaps one of the most famous locations in the region was Upper Dam. Sportsmen from all over the country knew of the tremendous brook trout caught every year from the pool located below the dam. The pool was generally fished from a Rangeley boat anchored in the fast moving current. During the last part of the 1800s, trout in excess of 10 pounds were caught in this spot. It was only natural that a major hotel was located on this site.

THE UPPER DAM HOUSE. The dam at the outlet of Mooselookmeguntic Lake was built in 1853 to aid in the movement of logs to the downstream mills. The original Upper Dam Camps were primarily used to house lumbermen; however, fishermen could find rough accommodations. The new Upper Dam House was constructed in the 1880s. A casino was constructed in the early 1920s. This impressive hotel operated until it was torn down in 1958, bringing a proud era to an end.

Six

PERSONALITIES

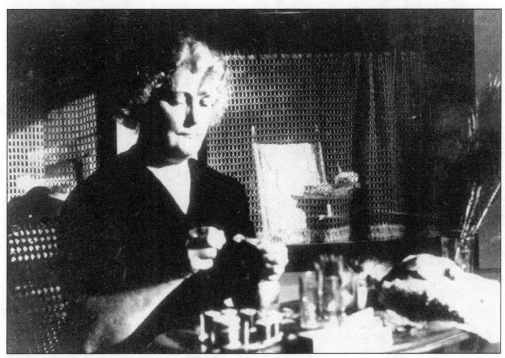

CARRIE STEVENS. A modest woman and milliner by trade, Stevens arrived at Upper Dam in 1919. She was to become perhaps the foremost female streamer fly tier. Over a period of 40 years, she created hundreds of streamer fly patterns that are coveted today by collectors all over the world.

GEORGE SHEPARD PAGE. In the early 1860s, George Shepard Page accompanied Henry O. Stanley on a fishing trip to the Rangeley Lakes region that was to forever change the region. Stanley's father had first visited Rangeley in 1840, discovering the incredible size of the brook trout. In 1863, Page made a second trip and returned home to New York with eight brook trout totaling $51^7/8$ pounds, an average of $6^1/2$ pounds each. The largest fish were presented to influential newspapermen who published accounts of the extraordinary trout. Then, an unprecedented excitement among anglers broke out. The famed Adirondacks had never yielded a brook trout that weighed five pounds. Thus began an influx of sportsmen that continues today. George Shepard Page was to become the first president of the Oquossoc Angling Association, an important part of the region's sporting history and tradition.

C. T. RICHARDSON. In 1862, C. T. Richardson purchased a cabin and land at Indian Rock at the confluence of Rangeley and Kennebago Rivers from Perley Smith. He built a larger camp and moved in with his family. He sold the property in 1865 to a group of sportsmen who soon formed the Oquossoc Angling Association. C. T. Richardson was to become its first superintendent.

GARRETT HOBART. In 1873, the family of Garrett Hobart built their own camp in the narrows between Mooselookmeguntic and Cupsuptic Lakes, where it is located today. Hobart was a leading New Jersey politician, head of the National Republican Party, and vice president of the United States under William McKinley in 1896. The family still occupies the camp.

ED GRANT. This legend of the Kennebago area was a guide, camp owner, fisherman, and teller of tall tales during the late 1800s. Grant is shown here in the back row, second from the right. His sense of humor and talent for exaggeration are illustrated in "The Tame Trout," a story of a trout he trained to follow him on dry land, until, as Grant reported, "Well sir, he followed me close up and came out onto the logs across the brook. . . . I heard a kee-plunk! behind me and Gorry! if he hadn't slipped through a chink between the logs and was drownded before my very eyes before I could reach him, so he was." Grant's lively sense of exaggeration extended to his advertising that proclaimed, "Ask anybody about Beaver Pond Camps and if they don't speak well of us, write us and we will."

Yours very truly,
F. C. Barker.

CAPT. FRED C. BARKER. A leading entrepreneur of the region was Fred Barker. He settled in the area in the 1870s, worked in a lumber camp, and was a river driver and trapper. Nicknamed "Trapper," he chose a life in the woods over an education, stating, "A man who could use an axe or cant dog, or handle a lumberman's bateau, was king beside the poor fellow who had to be enclosed in four walls figuring over long accounts in an office." In the spring of 1877, he purchased his first of many steamers, working out of the Oquossoc Angling Association. Four years later, with the arrival of the railroad, he bought the camps at Bemis Stream. He then opened more camps on Student's Island and finally built the much larger Barker Hotel. He wrote two highly sought after books, *Lakes and Forest as I Have Known Them* and *Hunting and Trapping,* coauthored with John Danforth. The books recount his exciting outdoor experiences. Barker's efforts as a businessman helped Rangeley become a major sporting destination.

CORNELIA "FLY ROD" CROSBY. Fly Rod's interest in the outdoors started when her doctor told her she would die if she did not get "abundant doses of fresh air," so she did. Fly Rod developed a passion for fishing and hunting in the Maine woods. It is reported that she and Annie Oakely did an exhibition shoot in Rangeley in 1905, although it is unclear who was the winner. As one of the first women to guide sports, Fly Rod became a proponent of local camps and of the licensing of guides. She received the guide license No. 1 for her efforts. Using her own celebrity and creativity, she promoted the region when she brought a log cabin, live trout, and trophy mounts from Maine to exhibit at Madison Square Garden. She also created a stir when she wore a costume whose skirt fell to a length eight inches above the ground, quite daring for the era. Her numerous publications on hunting and fishing in Maine attracted sports from all over the country. She lived to age 93, perhaps because of the abundant doses of fresh air she experienced.

J. WALDO NASH. One of the first major taxidermists in the region, Nash opened a branch office at Haines Landing c. 1900. In 1905, he patented a process for mounting the skin of a fish on a convex oval board. He eventually returned to Norway, Maine, when Walter Hinds took over his taxidermy shop.

WALTER HINDS. Starting his taxidermy business in Portland during the latter part of the 1890s, Hinds moved to Haines Landing accompanied by young taxidermist Herb Welch. Welch concentrated on fish, and Hinds concentrated on animals and birds.

HERB WELCH. Probably best known as the premier taxidermist of his era, Herb Welch created in his Oquossoc shop lifelike, realistic mounts of the trophies sportsmen caught in the Rangeley waters. Herb is shown here with a fine example of one of his mounts. He normally used a glass bubble to protect his work or mounted the fish on rectangular birch board with a stitched reed border.

WELCH'S ARTISTRY. Welch was an outstanding wildlife artist, especially when the subject was a favorite—trout or salmon. He was a sculptor, with one of his works reported to be part of the Louvre's collection in Paris. As a fly tier, he created a number of patterns well known to fly fishermen even today, including the Cupsuptic streamer, the Jane Craig streamer, the Yellow Jane Craig, the Kennebago streamer, the Welch Rarebit, and his most famous creation, the Black Ghost, a companion to Carrie Stevens's Gray Ghost.

HERB WELCH, TEACHER. Welch was also a teacher, as he enjoyed nothing more than sharing his knowledge and love for the outdoors with others, especially youngsters. Children in the Haines Landing area would come to his shop not only to learn how to cast or tie a fly, but also to learn about the wildlife and native plants in the local forest. He loved to teach his young admirers how to cast a fly and tell them stories that stirred their imaginations and stimulated their interest in the outdoors.

TED WILLIAMS AND WELCH. It is said that Welch taught Ted Williams to fly fish. They are shown here at a Boston sportsmen's show, along with an unidentified man on the left with Mr. and Mrs. Tom Yawkey, the owners of the Red Sox at the time.

PRES. HERBERT HOOVER. President Hoover and former Maine governor Lewis Barrows were guided by Herb Welch on their very successful trout fishing trip to Kennebago Lake. President Hoover was well known for his interest in fishing.

PRESIDENT EISENHOWER. Ike visited Rangeley as part of the centennial year in 1955. He fished at Little Boy Falls on the Magalloway River. In the first 15 minutes, he landed three trout, which he named Rhode Island, Connecticut, and Maine. All were released. Shown to the right of Ike are Welch and Sheldon Noyes. President Eisenhower was presented with a bronze of two leaping trout by Herb Welch.

CARRIE STEVENS (1882–1970).
A self-taught fly tier from Upper
Dam, Carrie created some of
the most beautiful and enduring
streamer patterns ever designed.
Her Gray Ghost streamer alone
would be enough to secure her a
place in fly-tying history.

The Rangeley's Favorite
Trout *and* Salmon Flies

Red Spotted Genuine Brook Trout, weighing
6 pounds and 13 ounces, taken at Upper Dam
by Mrs. Stevens, on one of her flies.

In ordering, give pattern number and size of
hook desired, and address

MRS. CARRIE G. STEVENS,

Upper Dam, Maine

CARRIE'S FLIES. Over 150
patterns that were originated
by Carrie have successfully
lured salmon and trout
from the Rangeley waters.
Collectors seek out original
Carrie Stevens streamer flies
and pay hundreds of dollars
for a fly that once sold for less
than $1.

The thought of loosing my large trout when it was nearly exhausted was too terriable to even think of. Expecting any moment my line would part, I was pondering on what would be the proper thing to do and deciding not to do anything for fear of making worse — with my line taut and not making a sound or move, I waited, and to my intense relief it came out and started away. Very carefully I worked it towards me and guided it out of the swift water, round to the side of the apron where I succeeded in getting it into the net and safely onto the apron — and oh, there was never anything so wonderful.

Not until my fish was safely landed did I realize the extent of my excitment, without waiting to remove the fly from the fishes mouth, — taking the fish and net in one hand and the rod in the other I rushed up to the hotel to have my fish weighed.

I am very proud, indeed, of catching such a nice large trout unassisted, and to win second prize in "Field and Stream Contest.

My trout weighed 6 lbs. 13 ozs. and is the largest trout taken in the pool for thirteen years.

It was taken with a Thomas Rod, Hardy Reel, Ideal Line and a fly I made,

Mrs. Carrie G. Stevens.

CARRIE'S ACCOUNT OF THE BATTLE WITH BIG TROUT. Shown here is rough draft written by Carrie Stevens recounting how she caught her now legendary 6-pound 13-ounce brook trout at the Upper Dam pool on July 1, 1924. She writes, "I made another cast and gave my fly three or four lively skips when this large trout struck it and dashed away at a terrific speed. I expected any moment it would run out all my line or reach the foaming white water before I succeeded in stopping it." Her fish, caught on a fly she tied and of her own design, won second place in the 1924 *Field & Stream* fishing contest. Perhaps more importantly, the publicity she received resulted in a flood of requests for some of her flies from fly fishermen across the country. Thus she began a career that was to make her one of the most famous fly tiers. Contrary to some reports, the fly pattern she used was Shang's Go-Getum, and not the Gray Ghost, which was to come later as her fly-tying style evolved. Because of the interest generated by her catch, Stevens was asked to write this account for a 1925 article in *Field & Stream*.

WALLACE STEVENS AND SHANG WHEELER. Carrie's husband, Wallace (right), is shown here receiving a gift from good family friend and artist Shang Wheeler. The poem is about the mythical trout "White Nose Pete" that was reputed to be the Upper Dam fish that always got away with the fly. Wheeler also carved a trout head that contained dozens of flies hooked in the mouth of White Nose Pete and presented it to Wallace.

DAVE FOOTER. A student of Herb Welch, Footer has become a master taxidermist and well-known artist, continuing in Welch's tradition. Shown on the right is Footer with Leslie Hilyard, an author and fly tier.

WALTER "SKEET" DAVENPORT AND DICK FROST. Local master guide and trapper Skeet Davenport gets the feel of a new fly rod in Dick Frost's shop at the top of City Hill. Frost is shown with some of the many flies he tied. He is well known for originating several streamer fly patterns, including the Blue Smelt.

KEN CROCKER ROD MAKER. Crocker started making fine split-bamboo fly rods in 1916. Using the best Tokin bamboo, which he seasoned for 25 years, he made the rods completely by hand. His signature, "hand made by K. C. Crocker," written in script near the rod butt, ensured a rod of the finest quality. Today, his rods are eagerly sought by collectors around the country.

LOUISE DICKINSON RICH. In her book *We Took to the Woods*, Louise Dickinson Rich recounts her adventures and shares her unusual way of life along the Rapid River during the late 1930s and the 1940s. Her stories include the spring log drive, wood and ice cutting, Christmas in the woods, and hunting and fishing when her family depended on the effort for food. Rich went on to write many books covering her experiences.

WE TOOK
TO THE
WOODS

Louise Dickinson Rich

WILHELM REICH. In 1943, noted analytical psychologist Wilhelm Reich purchased the Jesse Ross farm and established a research center. This controversial individual chose Rangeley and its pure air and healthy environment for his exploration of orgone energy, his work on the cloudbuster, and his child psychology experiments. Shown here is the place where he is buried at Orgonon, which remains open to the public.

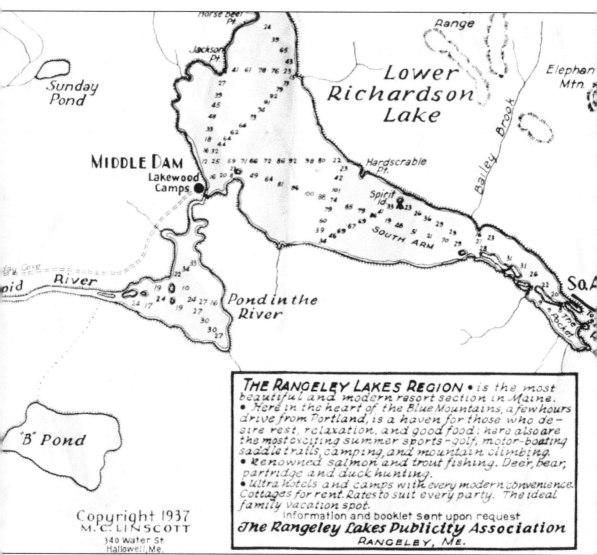

Copyright 1937
M. C. LINSCOTT
340 Water St.
Hallowell, Me.

A 1937 Map. This view of the Rangeley region in 1937 shows some of the surrounding communities. Bemis is located in the southeastern part of Mooselookmeguntic Lake. Oquossoc is at the northern part of Mooselookmeguntic, close to the western shore of Rangeley Lake. Kennebago is 10 miles north of Rangeley Lake.

94

Seven

BEMIS, OQUOSSOC, AND KENNEBAGO

MOOSELOOKMEGUNTIC AND CUPSUPTIC LAKES. At the western end of the Rangeley region lies two of its major lakes, Mooselookmeguntic and Cupsuptic. Taken from the top of Bald Mountain, this panoramic view is breathtaking. The village of Oquossoc lies near Haines Landing, seen behind the woman on the right, and the community of Bemis is to the left of this scene.

BEMIS. At the southern end of Mooselookmeguntic, the small community of Bemis boasted the only log railroad station in the country. The station was soon to become a victim of the all-so-common fire. A mill operated in the early 1900s and employed many workers. It also boasted a store built by R. B. Stratton, housing for the mill's employees, and a school. Bemis served as a departure point for Captain Barker's camps. In addition to the products of the mill, shipments of trout were sent to the markets in New York and elsewhere. A fire in 1921 destroyed 2,100 acres of Bemis woodland at a cost of $10,000 to the town of Rangeley.

Bemis Camps. Viewed from Mooselookmeguntic Lake is a portion of the community of Bemis. Note the expanded Camp Bemis and other buildings on the right. Shown on the far right is one of the boats used to haul log booms down the lake.

McKenzie Company. The store, originally built by R. B. Stratton and Charles McKenzie in Bemis in anticipation of the arrival of the railroad, was moved to Oquossoc when the village became the terminus for the railroad. It became known as C. H. McKenzie Company, later to become the Oquossoc Hotel.

R.R. STATION, OQUOSSOC, ME. 13.

OQUOSSOC. To reach the village of Oquossoc from Rangeley, travelers took a steamer to the Carry Road and walked a short distance to the village. However, the Rumford and Rangeley Railroad extended service to Oquossoc in 1902. Thus, the Rangeley region was served by two separate railroads, the standard-gauge train in Oquossoc and the narrow gauge in Rangeley. Oquossoc was ideally situated to serve the needs of the visiting sportsmen as they ventured forth to area camps. There grew up a number of stores, including Fred Fowler's store offering gifts, moccasins, souvenirs, and a wonderful ice-cream fountain that survives today as the Gingerbread House.

THE LOG CHURCH. Located on the Carry Road in Oquossoc, the Oquossoc Union Church reflects the rustic appearance of the village and is still open on a seasonal basis.

OUR LADY OF THE LAKES. The first Roman Catholic church was built in Oquossoc in 1909, largely as a result of the efforts of Cornelia "Fly Rod" Crosby, who was a recent convert to Catholicism. She was an energetic fundraiser who almost single-handedly raised the funds for the church.

MORTON'S MARKET. Ben Morton and his wife, Jo, began a small Oquossoc grocery store in the spring of 1939. Ben operated the store until he went into the service (from 1942 to 1945). After the building burned, they moved to the current site that had previously been a barbershop. They had assistance at the cash register from their young son, Scott, when he was two years old.

J. WALDO NASH, TAXIDERMIST. Located near Haines Landing in Oquossoc, this was one of the first taxidermy businesses in the area. Shown in this photograph are Herb Welch, on the left, and an unidentified man, possibly J. Waldo Nash or Walter Hinds.

W. D. HINDS, TAXIDERMIST. The Carry Road leading from Oquossoc to Haines Landing and Mooselookmeguntic Lake passed by the taxidermist store of Walter Hinds, originally occupied by J. Waldo Nash in the early 1900s.

HERB WELCH, TAXIDERMIST. Welch opened his own shop next to the Hinds building, where he concentrated on mounting fish. He later added a full line of sporting equipment and clothing to what became the center of outdoor sporting activity at Haines Landing.

KENNEBAGO LAKE. The Native Americans who were the lake's only regular visitors until the mid-1800s gave it the name Kennebago, meaning "sweet water." It is unclear when white settlers first visited the area, but trappers, hunters, and fishermen knew their way around the lake region. Kennebago lies 10 miles northwest of Rangeley. Approximately five miles long and one mile across at its widest point, the lake is more than 100 feet deep in some places. The nearby Canadian border made an attractive hideout for some reluctant conscripts, called skeddalers, during the Civil War. The area is still known as Skeddaler's Cove. The area remained remote with only the most adventurous sportsmen making their way to Kennebago.

GETTING TO KENNEBAGO. Arriving in 1891, the railroad brought increased numbers of sportsmen to the region. An 1896 edition of *Forest and Stream* magazine states, "One can leave New York at midnight and reach the village of Rangeley Maine the following afternoon at 6 o'clock, where in the interest of comfort, one must stay the night. . . . It will be necessary to engage guides at Rangeley to go to Kennebago Lake, as they do not stay at any of the camps. The ride on a springless buckboard to Kennebago baffles all description. The road could not possibly be worse if efforts had been made to make it so. It is filled with stones, rocks, boulders, holes, and the better way, and one practiced by a large proportion of the people, is to walk. But after one arrives at Kennebago the discomfort of the ten mile walk is soon forgotten. The hotel stands at the head of the lake, which is one of he most beautiful I have ever seen."

THE RAILROAD COMES TO KENNEBAGO. The Rumford Falls and Rangeley Lakes Railroad extended its tracks from Oquossoc to Kennebago in 1913. The train also provided fishermen access to the Kennebago River. Anna Bowditch relates a story of how her guide ran to the train returning to Kennebago and asked them to wait while she landed the large salmon she was battling. Visitors were met at the turntable and transported to camp.

GRANT'S CAMPS AT KENNEBAGO. In 1905, the Grant brothers, Will and Hall, along with their father, Ed, began Grant's Camps. Ed was instrumental in publicizing the region to sportsmen. He built a small log cabin, loaded the pieces on the train, and, along with Cornelia "Fly Rod" Crosby and others, entertained visitors at the Madison Square Garden exhibit in the 1890s. By the time Grant's Camps were built, he was famous for his tall tales.

A Steamer Trip to Camp. A steamer is shown here passing Grant's Camps to deliver its passengers and supplies to the Kennebago Lake House at the far end of the lake.

A Steamer at the Kennebago Lake House. This smaller steamer was well suited for traveling the long and narrow Kennebago Lake. Steamers were originally fired with wood and were later converted to coal. Tied up in front of the Kennebago Lake House, the steamer also served camps along the shoreline.

THE KENNEBAGO LAKE HOUSE CASINO. The hub of social life, the casino was built in 1914. Although there may have been some minor wagers placed on a game of cards, the casino was not a place for gambling, but the hangout for the increasing numbers of young people who spent all or part of the summer at Kennebago with their families. But the major attraction remained the outdoors.

KENNEBAGO GUIDES. In 1915, there were 27 guides working at the Kennebago Lake House with additional guides working at Grant's and private camps. The steamer would tow Rangeley boats to various fishing spots around the lake. From there, the guides would row their sports, take care of tackle, give advice, and handle the day's catch. Guests could also choose to take the steamer to the end of the lake and hop the train to be dropped off at the Kennebago River for a day's fishing.

SHORE LUNCH. Guides were famous for their shore lunches of trout and potatoes, or perhaps trout chowder, cooked over an open fire at one of several lunch grounds regularly maintained on the lake and river.

CAMPING OUT. Fishing adventures were also enjoyed at Little Kennebago and John's Pond for either the day or overnight. Youngsters especially enjoyed day hikes and fishing at Blanchard's Ponds and Flat Iron Pond. A favorite hike was to visit the fire tower on the top of West Kennebago Mountain. Visitors would take newspapers, magazines, and candy to the fellow whose summer job it was to watch for forest fires.

ELECTRICITY COMES TO KENNEBAGO. In 1916, a small electric plant, which was powered by glass-encased lead acid batteries, provided 200 lights that included one light that hung down from the center of each cabin. Grant's advertised that all their camps were lit by acetylene gas. Their daily rates were $2.50 to $4. Boats and canoes were 50¢ and a guide's board was $1.25.

KENNEBAGO GARDENS. Providing all the creature comforts for 100 guests at the Kennebago Lake House and 60 at Grant's was quite a job. Kennebago Lake House had a large vegetable garden and a flower-cutting garden. Chickens, cows, horses, and pigs were kept a distance from the camps. Grant's also advertised that they got daily shipments by trains of in-season fruits and vegetables and fresh meat. The area bootlegger made regular evening stops on the way back from Canada.

HAYING. Another important crop was hay to feed the livestock. Shown here are three unidentified men and a dog, posing in front of Kennebago Lake House camps.

RECREATION. Tennis was a favorite pastime of the era. The Kennebago Lake House held an annual tennis tournament among the guests, complete with a silver cup for the winner.

THE KENNEBAGO DIAMOND. In 1910, Fly Rod Crosby wrote in the *Maine Woods,* "Have you ever been to Kennebago? If not you should go, and if you have been you are sure to go again. Everyone knows, or should know, that Kennebago is one of the most beautiful of all the lakes in Maine. In fact, someone said, 'It is like a diamond surrounded by emeralds.' "

Eight

THE CITY

RANGELEY. The city, as locals referred to the center of commercial activity, is located on the northern side of the nine-mile-long Rangeley Lake, originally called Oquossoc Lake. It is conveniently situated along the route from Phillips and Madrid. In 1875, it boasted a population of 100, double the number of 20 years earlier.

WELCOME TO RANGELEY LAKES. The easiest access to Rangeley was an old trail that led from Madrid up the Sandy River valley, a rise of 1,000 feet, with mountain ridges on either side of the 13-mile trip to the head of the lake. Visitors were greeted by an arch over the road advertising local camps and hotels.

DOWNHILL TO THE CITY. Passing under the arch, visitors came down the hill leading to the city and its center of mercantile, lumbering, and outdoor sporting activities. This was the route used when traveling to Rangeley from Farmington and Phillips.

MAIN STREET. This scene shows Oakes, Quimby and Herrick; the Rangeley Tavern; and the Baptist church (in the distance). Note the buckboard and horse in front of the store.

Main Street Rangeley, Me.

ANOTHER VIEW OF MAIN STREET. The dirt road led through town, past retail stores and shops. Streets running to the left went to the lake, and those to the right led up the hill to residential areas.

MAIN STREET AND AUTOMOBILES. Here is a similar view of Main Street in later years, with early automobiles parked along the street on an angle. This parking was used until recently, when safety considerations led to the use of more conventional parallel parking.

WINTER IN THE CITY. The first snows were possible before the leaves turned color. It was not uncommon to have five feet or more of snow. The ground was often covered with white from October until May. Shown here is a snow-covered road heading to the lake, with the Rangeley Lake House on the hill in the background.

MAKING THE ROADS PASSABLE. Before the advent of motorized snowplows, the snow was rolled to allow the use of roads during the winter. Here, three teams of horses pull a large wooden roller that packs down the snow. When the roller was pulled up Cemetery Hill, youngsters often took advantage of the slow-moving roller by jumping inside and running against the rotating drum. The driver of the team chased the youngsters, only to have them try again.

THE SNOWPLOW. By 1930, progress had come to Rangeley in the form of a snowplow. The deep vee plow pushed the deep snow to the far edges of the road. In some years, the snow accumulation could exceed the height of a man.

WINTER TRAVEL. Once plowed, the roads quickly filled in with a new fall of snow, making driving difficult if not impossible. This road appears to be only wide enough for one-way traffic.

OXEN ON MAIN STREET. Four teams of oxen and two teams of horses pull a load of lumber down Main Street. When the dirt roads began to thaw in April, the roads became almost impassable and gave birth to the phrase "mud season."

ADVERTISING. This local advertising flyer announced the major mercantile businesses, including a boathouse, furnishings and footwear store, millinery, garage, livery, hotel, photography shop, bakery, steamboat company, trust company, and pharmacy.

THE RANGELEY TRUST COMPANY. Located on Main Street, the Rangeley Trust Company, built in 1905 by Harry A. Furbish, was the first commercial building built of bricks and mortar. It served as the only bank until it was replaced by a new bank building in 1922–1923. It was home to the town offices until 1979, when it was deeded to the Rangeley Lakes Region Historical Society.

THE NEAL, OAKES AND QUIMBY STORE. Shown are, from left to right, Will Quimby, Cell Schofield, Olin Rowe, Whit Butler, George Estes, and Walter Oakes. The progression of ownership is reflected in the names of the business. The store was originally known as Burke and Rogers in the 1880s, but changes in ownership resulted in an evolution of names, and it finally became Oakes and Badger (also called the "big store").

THE J. A. RUSSELL AND COMPANY STORE. The first local hardware store, J. A. Russell and Company, was started in 1886. It was located at the site of the present Rangeley Youth Theater. From left to right are Lurlene Ross McLafferty, Everett Scribner, John Russell, Lee Mitchell, Carol Berry, and Mason Russell.

PICKEL'S STORE. A local Rangeley taxidermist was Guy W. Pickel, who operated a sporting goods store from 1906 to 1926, although he mounted many animals and fish. After Pickel's death, his wife, Arbeth, continued the sporting part of the business.

THE MAIN STREET MARKET.
Howard Herrick, shown here, was the owner from 1916 to 1927 of the Main Street Market. It was located in the building that was originally the office of the area's first newspaper, *Rangeley Lakes*.

Rangeley Lakes.

VOL. 1.   RANGELEY, MAINE, THURSDAY, AUGUST 1, 1895.   NO. 10

RANGELEY LAKES. The first newspaper in the region was simply called *Rangeley Lakes*. It was started on May 30, 1895, and published until 1897. It continues to be a major source of information on this important time in the history of the area's growth. The editors and proprietors were Harry P. Dill and Elliot C. Dill. The subscription price was $1 per year, paid for in advance.

CROSBY'S GARAGE. Located behind the Rangeley Trust Company, Crosby's Garage served the needs of local residents and those visitors who toured to Rangeley for the season. Many touring cars and limousines belonging to summer residents were stored from September to June, including Packards, Marmons, LaSalles, Pierce Arrows, Cadillacs, and Duesenbergs.

THE JUNE 17 PARADE. A big event in Rangeley and the surrounding area was the June 17 parade, combining June 17 and Memorial Day celebrations. Right after World War I, Rangeley schoolchildren marched in the parade with American flags that were placed on the graves of local veterans. Honored veterans rode in an open touring car.

CIVIL WAR VETERANS. The last three Rangeley Civil War veterans, Eben Rowe, Dexter Lamb, and George Huntoon, appeared in many June 17 parades.

THE TELEPHONE COMPANY. The Dirgo Telephone Company took over service from the preceding telephone company, which dated from 1887. The new company took over a system with 34 telephones and 10 pay stations. The central office was in the Whitney Drug Store, but when the company was sold in 1909, the switchboard was moved to the second floor of E. V. Gile's store.

RANGELEY'S HAND PUMPER. Ready to go are the six members of the Rangeley Fire Company No. 1 that was formed on April 6, 1900. The hand pumper was a welcome addition to a community that lost so many buildings to fires including the Great Fire of 1876. That fire started in Luther Tibbett's mill at the base of City Hill and destroyed everything in its way to the outlet of Haley Pond.

THE SCHOOL BUILDING. In 1903, the town's growth was reflected in the construction of a large high school building. In the spring of 1911, the graduating high school class increased from two to four members. The building was destroyed by fire in 1911, rebuilt for the next year, and occupied for a spring term. However, on November 22, 1912, it burned for a second time. Arson was suspected but never proven.

THE FOOTBALL TEAM. The 1917 Rangeley football team poses for a photograph. From left to right are the following: (front row) Gale Ross, Conrad Lamb, Ois Brackett, Arno Spiller, and Kenneth Lamb; (middle row) Rex Hatch, Eddie West, Agis Oakes, Merle Brooks, Richard Herrick, and Lee Nichols; (back row) Dwight Lamb, E. P. Walton (the principal and coach), and Theron "Bill" Porter.

THE BASKETBALL TEAM. Seen is the 1918 girls' basketball team. The players are, from left to right, Elinor Moore, Muriel Brown Pillsbury, Pauline Rector, Everdeen Robbins Walden, Isabelle Russell, and Ormenta Corey.

THE RANGELEY PUBLIC LIBRARY. A lending library was first located on the second floor over the newspaper office. It later moved to the front portion of E. T. Hoar's fly rod shop and then to the outlet at Haley Pond before moving to its present site in 1909. The new building, constructed at a cost of $9,000, was largely a result of the financial support of summer residents. It contained 2,000 volumes.

THE MOVIE THEATER. Movies have a long history in Rangeley. They were shown in the Oakes and Badger hall in 1917. In 1923, Sherman Hoar's father, Anson, converted a grain shed located on marshy land into the Pavilion Theater, complete with a dance floor and stage. Moviegoers could hear the peepers and bullfrogs below during the silent movies. Seen here are, from left to right, the following: (front row) two unidentified men, Dorothy Bowles (piano player), and Arthur Nile (usher); (back row) Mabel Hoar (ticket taker), Harry Riddle and Sherman Hoar (owners), Carroll Doak (usher), and Percy Dennison (projectionist). In July 1930, talkies were introduced in the newly named Lakeside Theater. Walter Esley purchased the property in 1943 and continued operate it for almost 50 years, showing first-run movies to the summer visitors.

CANOEING ON THE SKI SLOPE. Dick Frost rode his canoe down the Saddleback Mountain ski slopes in the 1960s, during the annual Easter celebration. Frost worked at the mountain during the winter and guided and ran a sports shop for the remainder of the year. One of the first places to ski was at Rangeley Manor in the 1930s, then later at Hunter's Cove, and eventually at Saddleback Mountain.

THE WATER CARNIVAL. For many years in the 1930s, the Water Carnival was an annual event. It entertained visitors with motorboating, hydroplanes, a beauty pageant, canoe tilting, log rolling, and swimming races.

THE WEST RANGELEY BASEBALL TEAM. The local team was a champion of Franklin County in 1908. It consisted of P. Pillsbury, right fielder; G. W. Pillsbury, shortstop; G. Hoar, pitcher; D. Munyon, second baseman; Arlie Pillsbury, catcher; L. Hoar, left fielder; Dean Nile, center fielder; V. Mason, batter; and T. C. Haley, first baseman. This photograph was taken in front of the casino at the Lake House, where their games were played.

Doc Grant's Doll Carriage Parade. Elmer "Doc" Grant and his wife, Lelia, began a tradition in conjunction with the town's Fourth of July celebration that continues today. Local children decorated their bicycles, floats, and doll carriages with colorful banners and ribbons and paraded down Main Street to the town park, where the judging took place and prizes were awarded by Doc Grant.

"Thank You, Good Bye, Come Again." As visitors left the Rangeley Lakes region, they passed under this gate located near Salmon Ledge. It is hoped that readers have also enjoyed their tour of the early days of Rangeley's history, so thank you, good-bye, and please come again.

BIBLIOGRAPHY

Baldwin, Ruey Stevens, and Jim Eaton Hill, eds. *There Was A Land: Memories of Flagstaff, Dead River and Bigelow*. Eustis: Flagstaff Memorial Chapel Association, 1999.

Barker, Capt. F. C. *Lakes and Forest as I Have Known Them*. Lothrop, Lee and Shepard Books, 1903.

Calder, David. *45 Miles From Nowhere*. Performed by David Calder and the Yankee Soul Revue. Skowhegan, Maine: Cheapskate Sounds.

Ellis, Edward. *The Chronological History of the Rangeley Lakes Region*, 1983.

Farrar, Capt. Charles A. J. *Through the Wilds*. Estes and Lauriat, 1892.

Felton, Harold W. *The World's Most Truthful Man*. Dodd, Mead and Company, 1961.

Glimpse of the Great Pleasure Resorts of New England. G. W. Morris.

Hilyard, Graydon R., and Leslie K. Hilyard. *Carrie G. Stevens Maker of Rangeley Favorite Trout and Salmon Flies*. Stackpole Books, 2000.

Hunter, Julia A., and Earle Shettleworth Jr. *Fly Rod Crosby: The Woman Who Marketed Maine*. Tilsbury House, 2000.

Hutchinson, Doug. *The Rumford Falls and Rangeley Lakes Railroad*. Edited by Louise M. Korol. Dixfield: Partridge Lane Publications, 1989.

Ives, Edward D. *Joe Scott: The Woodsman-Songmaker*. Urbana: University of Illinois Press, 1978.

Kendall, William Converse. *The Rangeley Lakes, Maine; With Special Reference to the Habits of the Fishes, Fish Culture, and Angling*. Document No. 861. Department of Commerce, 1918.

Logging in the Maine Woods: The Paintings of Alden Grant. Edited by Margaret Yocom with Stephen Richard. Rangeley: Rangeley Lakes Region Logging Museum, 1994.

Martineau, Becky Ellis, ed. Letters of the John R. Toothaker family, 1890 to 1893. Typescript. Edwin Hamilton personal collection, Lisbon Falls, Maine, and Rangeley Lakes Region Logging Museum, Rangeley, Maine.

Masters of Photography. Farm Security Administration, http://www.mastersofphotography.com (December 16, 2003).

Priest, Gary N. *History of Rangeley Hotels and Camps*. Self published, 2003.

Scribner's Monthly, Volume XIII Trout Fishing in the Rangeley Lakes. Scribner Book Company, 1877.

Shirrefs, Herbert P. *The Richardson Lakes: Jewels in the Rangeley Chain*. Edited by Randall H. Bennett. Bethel: Bethel Historical Society, 1995.

Smith, David C. "A History of Lumbering in Maine, 1861–1960." *University of Maine Studies*, No. 93. Orono: University of Maine, 1972.

Smith, Robert. *My Life in the North Woods*. Boston: Atlantic Monthly Press, 1986.

Wood, Richard G. "A History of Lumbering in Maine, 1820–1861." *University of Maine Studies*, No. 33. Orono: University of Maine.

Yocom, Margaret, and Kathleen Mundell. *Working the Woods*. Rangeley: Rangeley Lakes Region Logging Museum, 1999.

Yocom, Margaret. Interviews with residents of western Maine. Personal collection, 1983–2003.